Between the Trees

Liam Scott

BookLeaf Publishing

Presentation by *BookLeaf Publishing*

Web: www.bookleafpub.com

E-mail: info@bookleafpub.com

ISBN: 9789357442633

First edition 2023

To Lucy, mum and my family.

Winter Haiku

With frost bitten bark,
His last leaf floats slowly down
Sleepy forest stream.

Sunrise Tanka

A fiery gold globe
Slowly rises from the sea,
Peering over clouds,
Torching the dark with the new,
Skies ablaze with beginnings.

Robin Haiku

The robin sits still,
In the tangled willows on
Misty riverbanks.

Absence

And smiling, did he pat you on the back?
Tell you that you'd done well, that he was
proud?
And would he stand by the sideline?
Tie loose, jacket slung, sleeves rolled up?
Would he berate you if you got there too slow?
Or maybe he said he'd let you one day, when
you're old enough.
And when you rang in 18 years, did he take you
to the nearest tap?
And laughing, would he see his laugh in yours?
Or maybe all he asked was for you to give your
best?
And that would be enough.
Or when he could no longer pick you up, or set
you down with ease, did his eyes meet yours?
And in them, would he see an equal then, or
something more?
And would he look up at you in awe, that you
were his, that he'd made you?

Did he lay foundations for the path you'll walk?
Did he give you his world so you can make your
own?

And if he did,
What was it like?

If I'm the frosts

If I'm the frosts of blood black Winter nights,
Then you're the thaw that morning brings.
If mine is in the cold, fast fading light,
Then yours is in the Spring.

Hazy Folds Haiku

The trees gently sway,
Sunlight falls in hazy folds
Through gaps in the wood.

Stand and stare

Try to listen closely,
let the silence speak,
the trees might whisper in your ear.
Stand and stare,
so you might feel the sea and sand between your
toes,
that you might see the sun bleed into the sky
when it sets.
Most moments are lost in time, unnoticed in the
rush.
Savour.

Lucy and Lauren's poem

Where other lights might fade and fail,
And fear paves the path ahead,
A sister's light can blaze the trail
With hands held tight at every end.

For Mothers

The silent laws all
Mothers make, bound in promise.
As strong as the oak,
Perennial as the oceans,
Devoted as the tides.

Still Water Haiku

Falling through the clouds,
Hazy yellow beams dancing
On the still water.

Seared Edges Haiku

Thrown in swirling fire,
The ink on the parchment fades
And the edges sear.

Goodness Haiku

Give goodness away
Like tall tree who loses his green,
It always grows back.

Anxious

Nothingness begins to spin,
Then roots and vines take hold,
Watered by my mind.

Modern Love - A Limerick

She was true and he was too,
Knew one another from back at school,
Then they kissed out on the piss,
And that then turned to nightly trysts,
They fucked it up and now they're through

When We're Apart

When we're apart, it's unknown and amiss,
A door without handles
or a box with no lid.

Blood Red Sky Haiku

Skies blood red, streaming
Like open veins, sun sinking
Beyond the eye's edge.

Spring morning Haiku

The spring morning clings
To winter's bitter harsh night,
Yet always, birds sing

Frozen Buds Haiku

The silvery bud,
That longed for sunlight, begins
To bloom towards it.

Milton Keynes UK
Ingram Content Group UK Ltd.
UKHW020647031023
429856UK00016B/659